MW01154056

Analyzing Data
in the
Jungle Park Case

Andrew Einspruch

First hardcover edition published in 2011 by
Capstone Press
151 Good Counsel Drive, P.O. Box 669, Mankato, Minnesota 56002.
www.capstonepub.com

This book was manufactured with paper containing
at least 10 percent post-consumer waste.

Editorial Credits
Sara Johnson, editor; Dona Herweck Rice, editorial director; Sharon Coan, M.S.Ed., editor-in-chief; Lee Aucoin, creative director; Rachelle Cracchiolo, M.S.Ed., publisher; Gene Bentdahl, designer; Eric Manske, production specialist.

Image Credits
The author and publisher would like to gratefully credit or acknowledge the following for permission to reproduce copyright material: cover Photo Edit/Tony Freeman; p.1 Photo Edit/Tony Freeman; p.4 Photolibrary Pty Ltd; p.5 Photolibrary Pty Ltd; p.7 Photolibrary Pty Ltd; p.8 Shutterstock; p.9 Photolibrary Pty Ltd; p.10 Getty Images Australia Pty Ltd; p.11 Shutterstock; p.12 Shutterstock; p.17 (left) Corbis Australia Pty Ltd; p.17 (right) Shutterstock; p.18 Photolibrary Pty Ltd; p.19 Pearson Education Australia/Michelle Jellett; p.20 Alamy/Pablo Paul; p.21 Shutterstock; p.23 Photo Edit/Tony Freeman; p. 24 Getty Images Australia Pty Ltd; p. 25 Photolibrary Pty Ltd; p.27 Getty Images Australia Pty Ltd; p.28 Shutterstock.

Library of Congress Cataloging-in-Publication Data
Einspruch, Andrew.
 Analyzing data in the Jungle Park case / by Andrew Einspruch.
    p. cm. -- (Real world math)
 Includes index.
 ISBN 978-1-4296-6616-9 (library binding)
 1. Crime--Juvenile literature. 2. Criminal investigation--Juvenile
literature. I. Title. II. Series.

 HV6027.E36 2011
 363.25'6--dc22
                        2010044636

Printed in the United States of America in Stevens Point, Wisconsin.
092010   005934WZS11

Table of Contents

What's Happening in Jungle Park?

Jungle Park is my favorite place in Greenville. Plenty of local kids have played there over the years. The park has a great jungle gym. So when a part of the jungle gym disappeared over the weekend, I was worried. When something else went missing two days later, I was upset. When another part went missing yesterday, I got mad!

This is Jungle Park before the crimes. After the first crime, a slide was missing!

The police were busy dealing with a bunch of serious robberies in town. They did not have much time for the Jungle Park case. So Hara and Hal (the H twins) and I figured that it was up to us to help solve the case. We would have to **investigate** the scene and collect the **evidence** ourselves.

The Scene of the Crime

The police **"freeze"** a crime scene. No one is allowed near the scene. It cannot be disturbed. Police and **forensic investigators** photograph the scene, collect data, and record what they see.

"Five Ws and an H," said Hara, as she looked at the damaged jungle gym. "That is what we have to figure out."

Hal wrote the 5 Ws and an H in his notepad. "Who, what, where, when, why, and how," he said.

"Well, *where* is obvious. *Where* is here at the park," I said. "And *what* is obvious too: pieces of the jungle gym are missing. That leaves *who*, *when*, and *how*."

Hal looked down at his notepad. "You left out the most interesting one: *why*. We need to figure out the **motive**."

Five Ws and an H

- Who?
- What?
- Where?
- When?
- Why?
- How?

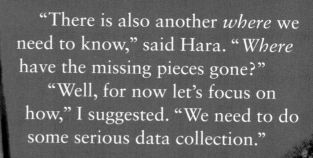

"There is also another *where* we need to know," said Hara. "*Where* have the missing pieces gone?"

"Well, for now let's focus on how," I suggested. "We need to do some serious data collection."

Children love the playground. We needed to act fast!

LET'S EXPLORE MATH

Jungle Park is very popular. This data table shows the number of children who played at Jungle Park over a 2-week period. Use the data table to answer the questions.

Mon.	Tue.	Wed.	Thu.	Fri.	Sat.	Sun.	Mon.	Tue.	Wed.	Thu.	Fri.	Sat.	Sun.
16	18	15	12	14	45	17	11	13	16	15	14	12	13

a. What is the total number of children who played at Jungle Park in the first week?

b. How many more children were at the park on the first Saturday than on the second Saturday?

c. Suggest a reason for this difference.

d. What is the range of the data? *Hint*: The range is the difference between the greatest and least values in a data set. You might find it helpful to order the data from least to greatest, then find the range.

It did not take long to figure out the *how*. Someone had used a **wrench** to remove the bolts from parts of the frame. Nuts and bolts were missing. There were scratches in the paint. These scratches looked new. They must have happened when the bolts were removed.

"There might be paint on the wrench that was used. That would be great evidence," said Hara.

LET'S EXPLORE MATH

Each month a park maintenance worker does a safety check to make sure that all the pieces of equipment in Jungle Park have the right number of bolts. Use the graph to answer the questions below.

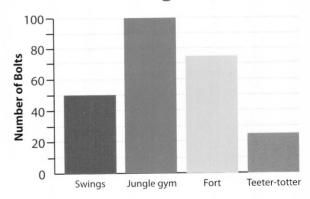

Bolts in Play Equipment at Jungle Park

a. Which piece of equipment has the most bolts?

b. In total, how many bolts are needed in all 4 pieces of equipment?

c. The maintenance worker counted only 45 bolts in the swings. How many new bolts do the swings need?

Hal found one of the bolts on the ground. He peered at the bolt, thinking. Suddenly, he leaped to his feet and jumped on his bike. He called over his shoulder, "Hold on! I will be right back."

Hara and I frowned as we watched Hal race away. We were both puzzled. While we waited, we searched the park for more evidence.

What to Do with the Data

Police and forensic investigators collect data at the crime scene. They put each piece of evidence in separate bags and containers. They then seal and label the bags. The evidence needs to be kept safe and organized.

Hara looked closely at the jungle gym. "Fingerprinting would not do much good," said Hara, rubbing her chin. "There would be hundreds of prints from everyone who plays here."

"Footprints too," I agreed, scuffing the ground with my toe. "There must be a thousand footprints here."

We kept looking but we could not find any useful data to help the case.

Whose Fingerprints?

Fingerprints at the crime scene might belong to the person who **committed** the crime. Fingerprints can be used to **identify** people because everybody's fingerprints are different. Every fingerprint has skin **ridges** that create a **unique** design.

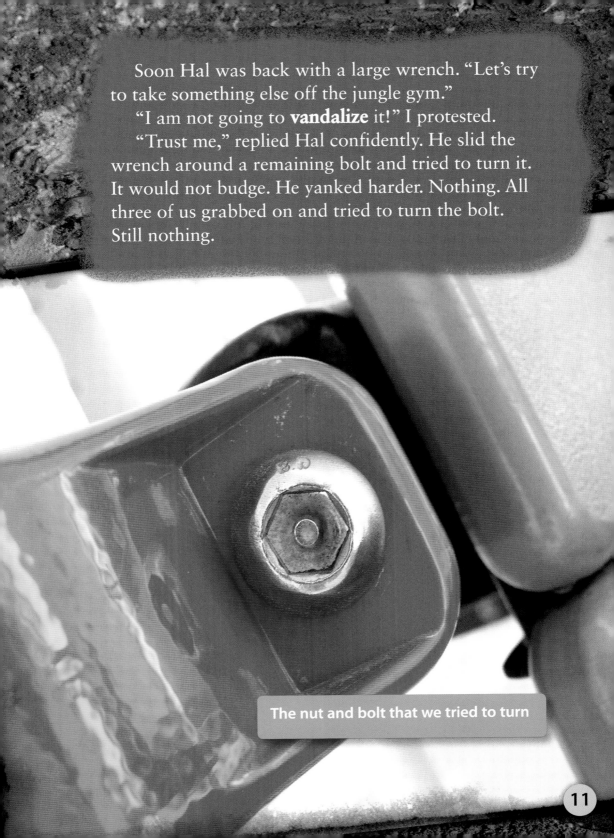

Soon Hal was back with a large wrench. "Let's try to take something else off the jungle gym."

"I am not going to **vandalize** it!" I protested.

"Trust me," replied Hal confidently. He slid the wrench around a remaining bolt and tried to turn it. It would not budge. He yanked harder. Nothing. All three of us grabbed on and tried to turn the bolt. Still nothing.

The nut and bolt that we tried to turn

"Just as I thought. Whoever did this must be strong," said Hal. "Or he or she used power tools."

"The police said no one heard anything," replied Hara. "Power tools would be noisy. So perhaps our **suspect** is male?"

"Maybe …" I mumbled. That is when I saw some tracks in the dirt. I pointed and said, "I did not notice those before."

I looked over at the H twins. "How much would the slide weigh?" I asked them.

Hal guessed, "Seventy pounds, maybe."

"That is pretty heavy," I replied. "These must be tire tracks."

"Of course—a car!" cried Hara. "You could hardly carry a big slide around, could you?"

"So our suspect has a driver's license," said Hal.

Crookville police found a set of tire tracks at a crime scene. The police looked at their **database** of tire tracks to try to find a match. A match would tell them who owned the car. Use the data in the table to answer the questions below.

Possible Suspects

Suspect	Tire Track Pattern	Tire Type
Mr. A.	thick tread, diagonal lines	car
Mr. X.	thin tread, crisscross lines	truck
Ms. Y.	thick tread, crisscross lines	truck
Mr. N.	thin tread, diagonal lines	car
Ms. O.	thick tread, diagonal lines	truck

a. The tracks had thick tread. Which suspects can be eliminated?

b. Further investigation showed that the tracks also have diagonal lines. Which suspect(s) can be eliminated now?

c. After researching tires, the investigators discovered that the tracks were made by truck tires. Who is your most likely suspect?

The Plan

The next day, we had lunch at Jungle Park. We talked about the data we had collected so far.

"We know it is likely a car was used," said Hara.

"We know there have been 3 separate thefts," said Hal.

"Each theft happened 2 nights apart. That might be a pattern," I added.

"It has been 2 days since the last theft, so there might be another theft tonight!" the H twins cried.

Data Collected So Far

- Likely a car was used

- 3 separate thefts

- Each theft happened 2 nights apart

We made a plan. We agreed an all-night **stakeout** of the park was the best idea. But we knew our parents would not allow it. So we decided our best chance of solving the case was to get some clear tire tracks. If more parts of the equipment were taken tonight, then there should be fresh tracks for us in the morning.

LET'S EXPLORE MATH

It is important to show data clearly. These two graphs show the same data. Both show the percent of various crimes that take place in Crookville at night. Use the data to answer the questions below.

a. Which crime has the highest percentage?

b. Which 2 crimes have the same percentage?

c. Which graph do you think best displays the data? Give your reasons.

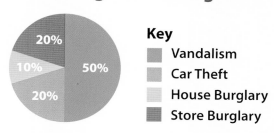

Crookville Crimes Taking Place at Night

Key
- Vandalism
- Car Theft
- House Burglary
- Store Burglary

Crookville Crimes Taking Place at Night

Later that day we prepared the area around the jungle gym for fresh data collection. We raked the ground. This cleared away all the leaves and the tracks that were already there. Next we watered the ground. Any tracks would be clearer on damp ground. Then we headed home for a tense night of waiting.

LET'S EXPLORE MATH

Many people visit Jungle Park. This graph shows the number of people visiting the park at certain times on a weekday. Use the data in the graph to answer the questions below.

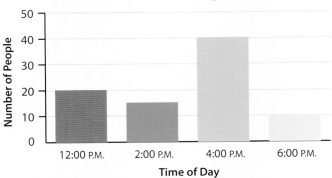

Visitors to Jungle Park

a. How many visitors were at the park at 2:00 P.M.?

b. What is the range of times when people visited the park?

c. The number of visitors was greatest at 4:00 P.M. Suggest a reason for this.

New Evidence

I met the H twins at Jungle Park early the next morning. Sure enough, another piece of the jungle gym was gone. The pattern had repeated.

There were some great tire tracks. We were pretty excited! The tracks were clear enough for us to make a **cast**. We got to work with some **plaster**. There were also lots of clear footprints. We made a cast of one of them too.

The plaster cast that we made of the tire track

Unique Shoeprints
The soles of shoes often have features, such as ridges, that make them distinctive. As the soles get worn, cuts and scratches can make shoeprints unique.

We proudly examined the casts we had made.

"One thing is clear," said Hal. "We have only found one set of footprints, so there was only one person. And that person wore some sort of hiking boots."

"Yeah," said Hara. "And the person is pretty big. Look at the size of the print. I think we are looking for an adult, or maybe a teenager."

Big Feet

Forensic investigators examine shoeprints to figure out the size of the shoe. Sometimes they can even figure out the brand of shoe.

"Look!" I pointed to the ground. "It is oil. The car has a leak. That helps narrow our search. We need to find a car with leaking oil and tires that match our cast!"

Hal picked up the cast of the tire tracks. "We need to talk to Bobo."

Bobo Donato runs Bobo's Tire Store. The store's motto is "We Never Tire of Tires."

The car oil we found at the park

Bobo Gives Us a Clue

Bobo looked closely at the cast of the tire track. "Good tire, that one," he said.

"You recognize it?" I asked.

"Please," he cried. "This is Bobo you are talking to! It is a RoadSnacker T-1100. I do not sell many of those. The tire has done about 3,000 miles, so it is still pretty new. The person drives a truck and brakes too hard. Whoever bought these knows all about tires. Plus the person likes licorice."

The three of us stared at him. We were stunned. "You can tell all of that?" Hal stammered.

The RoadSnacker T-1100 tires are used on large vehicles such as trucks and SUVs.

"Yep," Bobo replied seriously.
"But how did you know about the licorice?" I asked.
Bobo sipped his coffee and grinned. "I made that part up!"

LET'S EXPLORE MATH

This graph shows the sales of various tires at Bobo's Tire Store in one day. Use the data in the graph to answer the questions below.

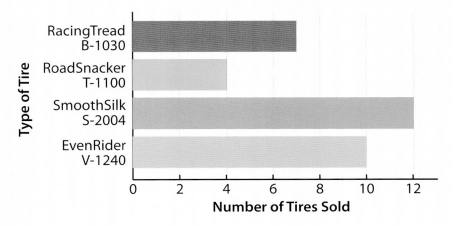

Bobo's Tire Sales

a. Which brand of tire is the best seller?

b. How many RoadSnacker T-1100 tires did Bobo sell in 1 day?

c. EvenRider V-1240 tires sell for $80 a tire. How much money did Bobo earn selling them?

d. Bobo identified the tire track as a RoadSnacker T-1100. He sold the least number of these tires in a day. Give a reason as to why this may help the children solve the case.

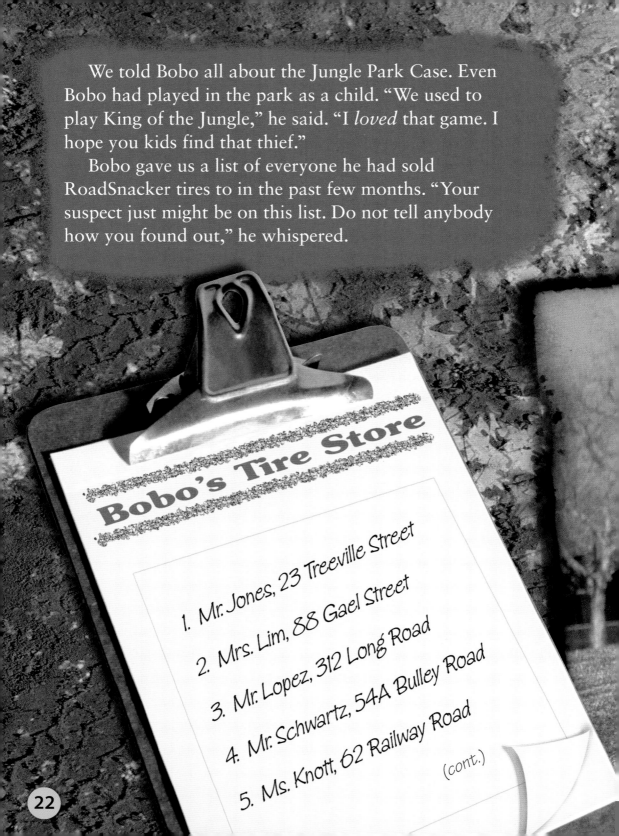

We told Bobo all about the Jungle Park Case. Even Bobo had played in the park as a child. "We used to play King of the Jungle," he said. "I *loved* that game. I hope you kids find that thief."

Bobo gave us a list of everyone he had sold RoadSnacker tires to in the past few months. "Your suspect just might be on this list. Do not tell anybody how you found out," he whispered.

Bobo's Tire Store

1. Mr. Jones, 23 Treeville Street

2. Mrs. Lim, 88 Gael Street

3. Mr. Lopez, 312 Long Road

4. Mr. Schwartz, 54A Bulley Road

5. Ms. Knott, 62 Railway Road

(cont.)

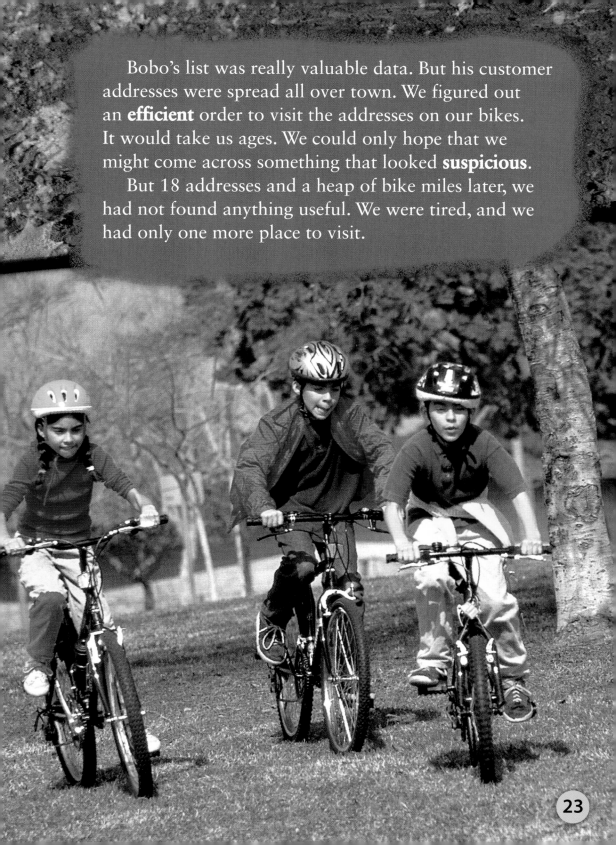

Bobo's list was really valuable data. But his customer addresses were spread all over town. We figured out an **efficient** order to visit the addresses on our bikes. It would take us ages. We could only hope that we might come across something that looked **suspicious**.

But 18 addresses and a heap of bike miles later, we had not found anything useful. We were tired, and we had only one more place to visit.

An Unexpected Ending

The last address was Chrissy Gastner's place. Chrissy was a girl from my class, but she had not been at school for a few weeks.

In the driveway was a pickup truck with a fairly new set of RoadSnacker tires. We got up close to compare the tires with our cast. We were sure the patterns matched. Then Hara spied something on the driveway.

"Oil leak!"

"This does not make sense," said Hal. "This truck belongs to Chrissy's brother, Doug. He is a nice a guy. Why would he steal pieces of the jungle gym?"

We heard a *clank* from the yard. It sounded like a wrench being dropped.

We looked over the fence. Everything fell into place. There was Doug reassembling the play equipment, wearing hiking boots. The boots looked like they would match our cast.

Finding a Suspect

Most criminals leave evidence, such as tracks, behind. But they can pick up evidence from a crime scene too! When police find a suspect, they can search the suspect's clothes and vehicle for soil. They may find dirt or rocks that match those at the crime scene.

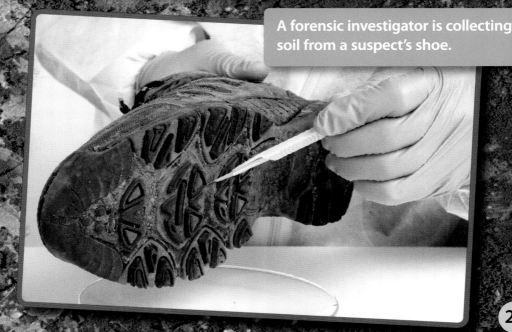

A forensic investigator is collecting soil from a suspect's shoe.

"Hey, Doug!" I called.

He jumped. And then he did something weird. He cried. Then he told us the whole story. Chrissy was really sick in the hospital. "She loves the jungle gym," said Doug. "I thought if she saw it when she got home, it might help her get better. I was going to return it."

We spoke to the police and the town council. Doug apologized and agreed that what he did was wrong. The police said Doug would have to do some community service.

LET'S EXPLORE MATH

Doug had to do 80 hours of community service. The circle graph shows the amount of time Doug spent on various jobs. Use the data to answer the questions below.

a. How many hours did Doug spend delivering groceries?

b. How many hours did Doug spend picking up litter and painting bus stop seats combined?

c. "Doug spent more time caring for hospital gardens than painting bus stop seats."

Do you agree with this statement? Use the data from the graph to support your answer.

Percentage of Hours Doug Spent On Various Jobs

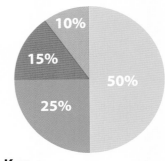

10%
15%
50%
25%

Key

- Caring for hospital gardens
- Delivering groceries
- Painting bus stop seats
- Picking up litter

The council members were understanding. So was our Greenville community. We did a fundraiser and managed to make enough money to buy a new jungle gym for Chrissy.

When Chrissy came home, the new equipment was in her yard to help her get better.

Case closed!

Stolen Gems

In Robberville precious gems have been stolen from a jewelry store. Crime scene investigators know that the criminal entered through a small window at the back of the store. The window is just over 7 feet above the ground. It is 24 inches wide and 24 inches high. They found a sample of type O blood. Yet there was no ladder that the robber could have used to climb up to the window.

This table is the data file for possible suspects.

Suspects	Height	Weight (lb.)	Body Shape	Blood Type
Mr. J.	6 ft. 4 in.	240	large	O
Mr. S.	4 ft. 1 in.	120	thin	O
Mrs. M.	5 ft. 3 in.	200	solid	A
Ms. D.	6 ft. 2 in.	135	thin	O
Mr. M.	6 ft. 2 in.	185	average	B
Ms. P.	4 ft. 4 in.	130	plump	O
Mrs. T.	5 ft. 1 in.	125	average	AB

Solve It!

a. Which suspect probably committed the crime?

b. Give reasons for your answer.

Use the steps below to help you find the data to justify your answers.

Step 1: A sample of blood type O was found at the crime scene. Make a list of the most likely suspects, based on this information.

Step 2: The window is just over 7 feet above the ground. Since there was no ladder, cross off the suspects who you believe could not have reached the window on their own. Explain your answer.

Step 3: The window was only 24 inches wide and 24 inches high. Look at the body shape and weight data of each suspect on your list. Cross off the suspect who you believe could not have fit through the window. Explain your answer.

Step 4: Look at your list of names. Which name is left? This name is your main suspect.

Glossary

cast—a molded shape made of plaster or another material

committed—carried out

database—a computer program used for storing information

efficient—best way to do something with the least amount of effort

evidence (EV-i-duhns)—information that can help you decide if something is true or false

forensic (fuh-REN-sik) **investigators**—people who look for evidence that will help police figure out who committed a crime

freeze—preserve; make sure nothing changes

identify—to figure out who someone is

investigate (in-VES-ti-gate)—examine or study carefully

motive—reason for doing something

plaster—a mixture of lime, sand, and water that dries hard

ridges—fine, raised lines

stakeout—a period of time when you watch something or someone carefully

suspect—a person the police think may have committed a crime

suspicious—not right; like it might have something to do with the crime

unique—the only one of its kind

vandalize (VAN-duh-lize)—damage or destroy on purpose

wrench—an adjustable tool for turning nuts and bolts

Index

ANSWER KEY

Let's Explore Math

Page 7:
a. 137 children
b. 33 more children
c. Answers will vary but could include that there was a birthday party held at the park or that it was a sunny day.
d. 45 − 11 = 34. The range is 34 children.

Page 8:
a. The jungle gym
b. 50 + 100 + 75 + 25 = 250 bolts
c. 5 new bolts

Page 13:
a. Mr. X. and Mr. N.
b. Ms. Y. **c.** Ms. O.

Page 15:
a. vandalism
b. store burglary and car theft
c. Answers will vary but circle graphs are appropriate for showing percents, or parts of a whole.

Page 16:
a. 15 visitors
b. 12:00 P.M. to 6:00 P.M. = 6 hours
The range is 6 hours.

c. Answers may vary but could include the fact that school has finished for the day and children are playing.

Page 21:
a. SmoothSilk S-2004   **b.** 4 tires
c. 10 x $80.00 = $800.00
d. Answers may vary but could include the fact that it narrows the list of suspects because it was not the most popular tire sold.

Page 26:
a. Delivering groceries: 25% of 80 hours = 20 hours
b. Picking up litter: 10% of 80 hours = 8 hours
Painting bus stop seats: 15% of 80 hours = 12 hours
8 hours + 12 hours = 20 hours combined
c. Answers will vary but should agree with the statement. The graph shows Doug spent 50% of his time caring for hospital gardens and only 15% of his time painting bus stop seats.

Pages 28–29:

Problem-Solving Activity

a. Ms. D. probably committed the robbery.
b. Ms. D. has blood type O. She is more than 6 feet tall; she could reach the window without a ladder. She has a thin body shape; she could easily have pulled herself through the small window.
Step 1: Mr. J., Mr. S., Ms. D., and Ms. P.
Step 2: Suspects Mr. S. and Ms. P. would be crossed off the list. They are both too short to reach up to the window and pull themselves through it.
Step 3: Suspect Mr. J. has a large body shape. He probably could not have fit through the small window.
Step 4: Suspect Ms. D. is left on the list.

DATE DUE

DEMCO 38-296